POWER FOOTBALL

THE **GREATEST** RUNNING BACKS

George Sullivan

Atheneum Books for Young Readers
New York London Toronto Sydney Singapore

PHOTO CREDITS: ALL "FOOTBALL CARD" PHOTOGRAPHS ARE USED COURTESY OF WIDE WORLD, EXCEPT FOR PAGES 40, 43, AND 52, WHICH ARE USED COURTESY OF GEORGE SULLIVAN.

Atheneum Books for Young Readers
An imprint of Simon & Schuster Children's Publishing Division
1230 Avenue of the Americas
New York, New York 10020

The text of this book is set in Century Old Style.

Printed in Hong Kong

10 9 8 7 6 5 4 3 2 1

Library of Congress Cataloging-in-Publication Data
Sullvian, George, 1933–
Power football / by George Sullivan.—1st ed.
p.   cm.
ISBN 0-689-82432-7
[1. Running backs (Football)—United States—Biography—
Juvenile literature. 2. Running backs (Football)—Rating of—
United States—Juvenile literature. 3. Football players.] I. Title.
GV939.A1 S89 2001
796.332/092/273 B21   00-045146

FIRST EDITION

Contents

Hard-charging Terrell Davis helped lead the Broncos to Super Bowl success. *(AP/Wide World Photos)*

Introduction

The job of the running back is to take a handoff or a pitchout from the quarterback and advance the ball by plunging into the line or trying to get around an end. From the other side huge linemen and quick and powerful linebackers try to slam that runner to the ground. Running backs have football's toughest job.

Running is instinct, something a player is born with. You don't teach running. That speed, all those cuts, fakes, and changes in direction, are based on natural talent.

"I was never taught to do what I did and I know I couldn't teach anyone else how to run," Red Grange, the great running back of the 1920s and 1930s, told Paul Zimmerman in *A Thinking Man's Guide to Pro Football.* "I don't know what I did on any individual run."

Running backs are sometimes asked to block, clearing the way for another ballcarrier, or they will be called upon to pass block—that is, defend the quarterback. And they are also used as pass receivers, circling out of the backfield to take the quarterback's soft tosses.

The workhorse of the dominating Dallas Cowboys during the 1990s, Emmitt Smith set a helmetful of NFL records. *(AP/Wide World Photos)*

But carrying the ball, advancing it, is what's vital. Blocking and pass receiving are secondary assignments.

Why is running so important? A team that can't run the ball successfully can't win. It's as simple as that. Passing is important, of course; in fact, it often plays a crucial role. But a team that can't move the ball effectively on the ground usually won't have much of a passing game. Basic football strategy dictates that a team must seek to establish the run, get the running game humming, before attempting to pass. Running lays the foundation for passing. It is almost never the other way around.

In Super Bowl XXXII in 1998 the Green Bay Packers were set up to stop the passes of Denver's John Elway, the best quarterback of the time. But the Packers were so focused on defending against the pass, they were surprised to get buried by the running of Terrell Davis, who gained 157 yards, a Super Bowl record. He scored three rushing touchdowns, also a record. The underdog Broncos won, 31-24.

Bill Parcells, coach of the New York Jets during the late 1990s, was once discussing the importance of Curtis Martin, the team's number one runner. The Jets got Martin from the New England Patriots in 1998. Once Martin had become a member of the New York team, Parcells stressed the importance of having him gain one hundred yards or more in a game. "If you have a back rush for one hundred yards," Parcells said, "you're going to win seventy percent of the time." Statistics showed Parcells's theory to be true.

Barry Sanders of the Lions spent his career eluding tacklers with his fancy cuts and spins. *(AP/Wide World Photos)*

Nicknamed "Sweetness," Walter Payton is often hailed as the greatest running back of all time. *(AP/Wide World Photos)*

Running the football was not always as essential as it is today. In the beginning football was not a running game, nor was it a passing game; it was a kicking game. Up until the 1880s football resembled rugby, a game in which a pair of teams seek either to kick or to carry the ball toward the opponent's goal line. There was no professional football at the time, incidentally. Football was only played in schools and colleges.

In 1882 the concept of downs was introduced. Forward passing became legal in 1906. But coaches shunned the pass at first. It was considered too risky. When the American Professional Football Association, the first pro league, came into existence in 1920, running the ball was still the chief form of attack. (The APFA renamed itself the National Football League, the NFL, in 1922.) Running backs were the professional game's first superstars.

Pro football at that time was a pathetic business. It was practically ignored by sports fans. Baseball, boxing, and college football were the popular sports. The NFL was a collection of scruffy, ragtag teams. While there were franchises in a handful of big cities of the East and Midwest, such small towns as Pottstown, Pennsylvania, and Rock Island, Illinois, were also represented. Rosters changed from week to week. Except for a few former college stars, players were paid from twenty-five to fifty dollars a game. Most worked at other jobs during the week. Schedules were haphazard, with owners arranging games on the spur of the moment. No team prospered. Clubs struggled simply to stay alive.

On the field it was a rough game, populated by two-way players. In other words, when a team on offense gave up the ball, the players on the field shifted over and played defense. Running backs took over as defensive backs. A center or guard might become a tackle. These were sixty-minute players.

It wasn't until the 1930s that pro football became an established sport. New rules opened up the game and sped it up, too. There were more field goals, more passes, and more points scored. Sellout crowds remained a rarity, however. Survival was still every club's ambition.

With the 1940s came an even greater emphasis on speed and quickness. Running backs became faster and more elusive. Passers were more accurate and receivers more sure-handed. In 1949 pro football introduced free substitution. Few players played two ways; many played only one position. Thus, each player could now fine-tune his specialty.

Through the decades players who primarily run with the football have been designated either half-backs or fullbacks. They are both running backs, of course.

The fullback lines up three or four yards behind the quarterback. He is usually bigger and more powerful than the halfback. The job of the fullback is to pound hard up the middle: get the tough yards.

Where the halfback lines up depends on the formation that the team is using. In the I formation, for example, the two running backs line up in back of each other behind the quarterback. The halfback is the man in the middle.

Football formations used to include two halfbacks, not merely one. Then coaches began using one of the halfbacks chiefly as a pass receiver. The man would be split out to the right or left so it would be easier for him to get past the line of scrimmage. The position became known as split end or flanker, then wide receiver or wideout. As these changes in terminology were developing, fullbacks and halfbacks were more generally becoming referred to as running backs.

This book profiles the best of these specialists from the present as well as the past. Each was the top runner of his time. As in any book of this kind, some possibly deserving players have been left out. Larry Csonka, Jim Taylor, and Steve Van Buren are some names that quickly come to mind. To their fans, I apologize. The players that are covered were preeminent not only as running backs; each was famous enough to attract the attention of the public in general, not just football fans or sports enthusiasts. Each was the type of celebrity who would be pictured in *People* as well as *Sports Illustrated*. In many ways, each of these runners had an impact not only on his team's performance, but also on the game of football in a broader sense.

Terrell Davis

Born: October 28, 1972; San Diego, California
Height: 5' 11"   Weight: 210 lbs.
High School: Abraham Lincoln (San Diego)
Colleges: University of Georgia; California State University Long Beach
Pro Team: Denver Broncos, 1995–

There are days when Terrell Davis is unstoppable. Take Super Bowl XXXII in 1998 as an example. Davis's team, the Denver Broncos, faced the Green Bay Packers.

In the first quarter Davis used his speed and power to rip through the Green Bay line, then cut back against the flow of the play for huge gains. Before the period ended, Davis blasted into the end zone for the game's first touchdown.

As the second quarter began, Denver had the ball on the Green Bay one-yard line. Davis had been kicked in the helmet late in the first quarter. The blow had caused his vision to blur. Denver coach Mike Shanahan asked Davis how he was feeling.

"I'm seeing double and triple," Davis said.

Shanahan decided to use Davis as a decoy. "Go over the top," he told him.

Quarterback John Elway faked a handoff to Davis. As the Green Bay linemen swarmed toward Davis, Elway skirted around the right end for the touchdown.

Davis also excels as a pass receiver. Here he tumbles into the end zone following a reception against the Seattle Seahawks.
(AP/Wide World Photos)

Davis sat out the rest of the quarter. But after the halftime break, Davis's vision had returned to normal. He went back into the game to help destroy the Packers.

His one-yard touchdown plunge with one minute

forty-five seconds remaining in the game earned the Broncos a 31–24 upset victory. Davis carried the ball thirty times for 157 yards. He scored three touchdowns to set a Super Bowl record and was voted the game's Most Valuable Player.

Afterward, Elway praised Davis, not only for his Super Bowl performance, but also for what he had done all season long. "Since he's been there, my job is to basically pick up third downs, to keep him on the field so that I can hand him the ball," the quarterback said. "We get there on his back."

The next year, 1999, the Broncos were back in the Super Bowl. Davis had enjoyed a banner season. He ran over every team that the Broncos faced. He rushed for 2,008 yards, becoming only the fourth runner in history to gain 2,000 yards or more in one season. (Eric Dickerson ran for 2,105 yards in 1984, and Barry Sanders for 2,053 yards in 1998. O. J. Simpson had 2,003 yards in 1973.) His remarkable running skills earned Davis the NFL's Most Valuable Player award.

In Super Bowl XXXIII, Denver faced Atlanta. The Falcons went into the game with a defensive plan that was intended to stop Davis. But he still managed to gain 102 yards on twenty-five carries. The Broncos romped to a 34–19 win.

After the game it was revealed that Davis had suffered a painful groin injury the previous week. It had been kept a secret. But Davis played, and played hard.

"He would never admit it, but his groin was killing him," said Denver running back Derek Loville. "It was very painful."

In the fall of 1999, Davis was ready to carry the Broncos to a third straight Super Bowl. But early in the season in a game against the New York Jets, Davis angled in to make a tackle following an interception. In a collision at the play's end Davis suffered what could have been a career-ending knee injury.

But Davis didn't disappear. He seemed to thrive on the pain and hard work of rehabilitation. By the spring of 2000 he was ready to resume his role as the Broncos' leader and the game's best running back.

Surviving is part of Davis's character. Growing up in one of San Diego's roughest neighborhoods, he had to be tough to pull through in spite of the drugs and crime that surrounded

Davis's friends and teammates admire his toughness and determination to do well even when hurting. *(AP/Wide World Photos)*

Davis runs fast and hard. Here he drives for short yardage against the Kansas City Chiefs. *(AP/Wide World Photos)*

him. Instead of taking up with a gang, Terrell turned to football. As an eleven-year-old, he carried the ball for the Valencia Saints in a Pop Warner league.

"Even then, Terrell was something," Reuben Fears, his first coach, once recalled. "You knew he was going to be good. He made us all proud."

Terrell lived about a mile and a half from Abraham Lincoln High School, where the Pop Warner teams practiced. When he played in his first Super Bowl at Qualcomm Stadium in San Diego, Terrell wasn't far from his old backyard.

Later he played for the University of Georgia, but injuries hampered him there. He also continued to suffer from throbbing migraine headaches, which had plagued him since his childhood.

Davis carries the ball in the AFC Championship in Denver in 1999. Davis rushed for 167 yards and one touchdown. Broncos won, 23–10. *(AP/Wide World Photos)*

Terrell was virtually unknown as a college player. The Broncos took a chance on him, drafting Terrell after 195 other players had been picked.

Terrell was thrilled. "When Denver drafted me," he said, "I was just hoping to make the practice squad."

After all, Denver already had John Elway, one of pro football's all-time great quarterbacks. They had a defense that could stop the run and put pres-

sure on the passer. They had special-teams players that could beat you in the blink of an eye. In Mike Shanahan they had one of the game's best coaches, adept at play calling and attacking opposition weaknesses. How could an unheard-of player fit in?

It turned out that Terrell Davis was the final piece of the puzzle. When he was his unstoppable self, making the big plays, everything else opened up. The years of Super Bowl glory quickly followed.

Barry Sanders

Born: July 16, 1968; Wichita, Kansas
Height: 5' 9"   Weight: 200 lbs.
High School: North (Wichita)
College: Oklahoma State University
Pro Team: Detroit Lions, 1989–1998

Great runners have their own style. Eric Dickerson ran on instinct, dipping, rolling, and spinning through NFL defenses. Gale Sayers slashed through the line, then exploded away. Walter Payton attacked would-be tacklers.

Barry Sanders was different. He followed no pattern. He was creative, making it up as he went along. Football people called him a "freak runner." Like a human pinball, he caromed off tacklers, cutting and twisting, bumping and spinning, and then he was gone.

"He takes your breath away," said his college coach at Oklahoma State.

Hall of Fame running back Gale Sayers also marveled at Sanders's talent. Said Sayers: "How many times can you remember looking at a player,

Sanders led the NFL in rushing three times, and in 1997 became the third runner in history to rush for 2,000 or more yards in a season. *(AP/Wide World Photos)*

9

Sanders lands in the end zone after
a pass reception against the New York Jets.
As a receiver, Sanders averaged more than 30 catches a season.
(AP/Wide World Photos)

whether it's a quarterback, running back, or line-backer, and saying, 'I've never seen that done on a football field before.' With Barry it happens every game, and in some games almost every time he touches the ball."

Sanders used his light-footed skills to earn some glorious statistics. At Oklahoma State he won the 1988 Heisman Trophy as the best player in college football. He arrived in Detroit to play for the Lions in 1989. That year he rushed for 1,470 yards and was named Rookie of the Year. He went on to become one of the NFL's elite runners, winning four rushing titles. He never rushed for fewer

than 1,100 yards in a season. In 1997, with 2,053 yards rushing, he became the third back in history to rush for 2,000 yards in a season. He was named the league's Most Valuable Player that year.

Sanders was always very modest about his achievements. After he won the Heisman Trophy, he was invited to visit the White House to meet President Ronald Reagan. Sanders turned down the invitation. He said he had to study.

Sanders "never keyed on records," as he himself put it. In the final game of the 1989 season Barry was within ten yards of surpassing Christian

Okoye of the Kansas City Chiefs and winning the league rushing championship. Detroit coach Wayne Fontes asked Barry whether he wanted to go back into the game and try to top Okoye. Sanders shook his head. "Let's just win and go home," he said. Okoye won the rushing title.

Although Sanders was a great individual success, the Lions seldom won consistently in his years with the team. Coaching changes and quarterback changes hampered the team. Poor choices in the football draft also hurt. In Barry's ten years with Detroit the team won only one play-off game. The Super Bowl? The Lions never got close.

All of the losing seasons weighed heavily on him. He got sick of the Lions and sick of football. As the 1999 season approached, Sanders was only 1,458 rushing yards from becoming pro football's all-time rushing leader. That's how many yards he

As a member of the Lions, Sanders was looked upon, in the words of a rival coach, as "the key that made everything go." *(AP/Wide World Photos)*

Sanders takes a break on the Detroit bench during a loss to the Chicago Bears in 1994. *(AP/Wide World Photos)*

needed to beat Walter Payton's record of 16,726 yards. Sanders loomed as the first running back to rush for 20,000 career yards.

It never happened. Just one day before the opening of Detroit's training camp in 1999 the thirty-one-year-old Sanders announced that he was retiring. "The reason I'm retiring is simple," he said. "My desire to exit the game is greater than my desire to stay in it."

Some observers thought that Barry would reconsider his decision. Others thought he would accept a trade and play for another team.

But Barry stuck with his decision. He was fed up. He had lost his passion for the game. It was time to go.

Emmitt Smith

Born: May 15, 1969; Pensacola, Florida
Height: 5' 9"   Weight: 200 lbs.
High School: Escambia (Pensacola)
College: University of Florida
Pro Team: Dallas Cowboys, 1990–

During the 1990s, the Dallas Cowboys often won by putting the ball in Smith's hands. Above, Smith runs for daylight against the Chicago Bears. *(AP/Wide World Photos)*

"A complete grinder." That's what they call Emmitt Smith. He'll do whatever he has to do to make the Cowboys win.

"I don't think that there's a selfish bone in his body," Joe Brodsky, the running-back coach of the Dallas team, once said. "He'll give it all up—everything—for the team."

When the Cowboys met the New York Giants in the final game of the regular season in 1993, Emmitt was hurt. He had a partially separated right shoulder.

But Emmitt refused to watch from the sidelines. The game was too important. The division title was at stake. Despite the bad shoulder, Smith charged into the Giants' line again and again. The Cowboys won, 16–13.

Smith played tough in the pair of play-off games that followed, and the Cowboys won them both. They then faced the Buffalo Bills in Super Bowl XXVIII. Smith was still hurting, but it didn't seem

Smith is congratulated by Kevin Gogan after scoring a touchdown against the Buffalo Bills in Super Bowl XXVIII, won by Dallas, 30–13. Smith was the game's MVP. *(AP/Wide World Photos)*

seem to matter. He was fearsome, rushing for 132 yards and scoring two touchdowns. The Cowboys crushed the Bills, 30–13.

Smith was voted the game's Most Valuable Player. Earlier he had been named the league's MVP for the regular season. Emmitt Smith was the first player to claim both honors in the same season.

There were many more prizes in the years that followed. After ten seasons with the Cowboys, Smith had three Super Bowl rings and four rushing titles. In 1992, with 1,713 yards rushing, Emmitt gained more yards than fifteen NFL *teams*. He scored 136 touchdowns in those ten years,

making him the all-time rushing touchdown leader. Not bad for a grinder.

Scoring touchdowns is kind of a habit with Emmitt. In 1995 he scored a record twenty-five touchdowns. Sports experts compared that feat with the record 4,029 points that Wilt Chamberlain scored in the 1961–62 season in the National Basketball Association and the ninety-two goals that Wayne Gretzky scored in the 1981–82 National Hockey League season.

Whether scoring touchdowns or streaking for long gains, Emmitt brings excitement to the game. "You look at Emmitt and think something special might happen at any time," said Tony Dorsett, a Hall of Fame runner for the Cowboys. "He keeps you on edge."

Following his record-breaking performance in 1995, Emmitt had some difficult seasons. All the hits that he had taken caught up with him. He was worn out and his body ached in a hundred places.

At one time or another he was being treated for injuries to his neck, ribs, ankle, shoulder, and knee.

Emmitt was no longer able to move piles of players with his bull-like rushes. The leaky Dallas offensive line was part of the problem. Rushers zoomed right through to nail poor Emmitt just as he was getting started.

Change came with a new coach. By 1999 it was obvious that the old Emmitt was back. He was the team's dominant player once more. With his 1,397 yards rushing, Smith achieved his ninth straight season of rushing 1,000 yards or more. Barry Sanders is the only other running back to accomplish that feat.

"I think of being the greatest," Emmitt said early in his career. "I think about it all the time. I'm chasing after legends, after Walter Payton and Tony Dorsett and Jim Brown and Eric Dickerson."

In the latter stages of his career Emmitt began surpassing the all-time records held by these and other great runners. Eventually there was almost no one left for him to chase. And the NFL's younger runners were chasing Emmitt Smith.

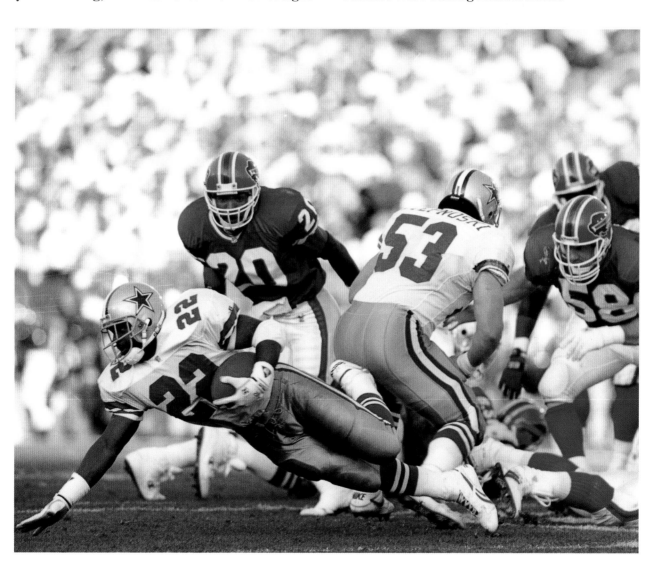

Smith stretches for yardage against the Buffalo Bills in Super Bowl XXVII in 1993. Cowboys buried Bills, 52–17. *(AP/Wide World Photos)*

Eric Dickerson

Born: September 2, 1960; Sealy, Texas
Height: 6' 3"   Weight: 220 lbs.
High School: Sealy
College: Southern Methodist University
Pro Teams: Los Angeles Rams, 1983–1987;
Indianapolis Colts, 1987–1991; Los Angeles
Raiders, 1992; Atlanta Falcons, 1993
Entered Hall of Fame in 1999

Eric Dickerson exploded upon the pro football scene in 1983, drafted by the Los Angeles Rams following an outstanding career at Southern Methodist University. There he had shattered Southwestern Atlantic Conference rushing records.

It didn't take Dickerson long to make his mark as a professional. A gliding, sliding runner with the power to bury tacklers when he had to, Dickerson carved out one hundred-yard game after another as a rookie. In some games he was especially awesome. He rushed for 192 yards in a game against the New York Jets, 199 yards against the Detroit Lions.

By the end of his rookie season Eric was a star. He led the NFL in rushing that year, with 1,808 yards. He carried the ball a record 390 times. No one was surprised when he was named Rookie of the Year.

Dickerson was just warming up. The next season, 1984, he reached a pinnacle with his slashing running style. He gained 2,105 yards, topping O. J.

Dickerson poses in Rams's locker room in 1983 after learning that he had been named NFL Offensive Rookie of the Year. *(AP/Wide World Photos)*

Simpson's single-season rushing record of 2,003 yards, and was named the league's Most Valuable Player. Some people hailed him as the best running back of his time, and this was a time when there were people like Walter Payton, Marcus Allen, and Tony Dorsett carrying the football. In 1985 and 1986 Dickerson continued his streak. In all, he gained 1,200 yards or more in each of his first four pro seasons.

But Dickerson was not happy. He felt that he was underpaid. He called an executive with the Rams "an eel" and led the league in whining.

During the 1987 season Los Angeles traded Dickerson to Indianapolis for a large number of players and draft choices. Maybe a change in scenery would be good for Eric, people thought.

With Indianapolis, Dickerson continued to grind out yardage in very big chunks. By 1989 he had crossed the ten thousand mark in career rushing yardage. He had gotten there in only ninety-one games, fewer games than anyone else—seven fewer than Jim Brown and nineteen fewer than O. J. Simpson. Dickerson also became the first player to rush for one thousand yards or more in seven consecutive seasons.

Still, there were problems. Dickerson missed practices and was suspended. He complained and complained. He said that he didn't like football and threatened to quit. By this time many fans had

After a long run, Dickerson holds the ball high to signal a touchdown. *(AP/Wide World Photos)*

After being traded to the Colts, the goggle-wearing Dickerson continued to perform as one of the game's most dangerous runners. *(AP/Wide World Photos)*

17

grown to dislike him. They felt that he was interested only in money, not the team, not winning. He was often loudly booed. Once, when he took the field for a game at Anaheim Stadium, Rams fans threw Monopoly game money at him. Eric didn't seem to mind. "If they had thrown real money, I would have picked it up," he said.

During the early 1990s, Dickerson bounced around from the Colts to the Raiders and, finally, to the Falcons. In 1993, after a dreary season with the Falcons, he did quit.

At the time, Dickerson ranked third on the all-time rushing list with 13,259 yards, behind Walter Payton and Barry Sanders. He called his single-season rushing record of 2,105 yards his greatest accomplishment.

Rushing records are what Eric Dickerson has to show for his career. He never played in a Super Bowl; he never got close. In 1999 he was thrilled to learn that he had been voted into membership in the Pro Football Hall of Fame. "This is my Super Bowl," he said.

When he retired in 1993, Dickerson, with 13,259 yards, ranked as the NFL's second all-time leading rusher. *(AP/Wide World Photos)*

Marcus Allen

Born: March 26, 1960; San Diego, California
Height: 6' 2"   Weight: 210 lbs.
High School: Abraham Lincoln (San Diego)
College: University of Southern California
Pro Teams: Los Angeles Raiders, 1982–1992;
Kansas City Chiefs, 1993–1997

If the National Football League ever developed a statistic for toughness, Marcus Allen would be the all-time leader. During his sixteen-year career with the Los Angeles Raiders and Kansas City Chiefs, Allen established himself as the game's guttiest and most durable running back, a player with an intense desire to play and win.

"Marcus is like something out of a Monty Python movie," said Allen's teammate Howie Long, an all-pro defensive end for the Raiders. "You cut the guy's leg off, he keeps coming. You cut his other leg off, he's still coming. You cut off his arms, chop up his torso, and he keeps after you."

Marcus Allen's toughness and pride carried him to a spectacular career. He won every major award in high school, college, and professional football.

At Abraham Lincoln High School in San Diego, where he started out as a free safety and later switched to quarterback, Allen was named California

Allen went to the University of Southern California because his idol, O. J. Simpson, went there. Above, Allen breaks a tackle in a game against the University of Oregon in 1980, his junior year at USC. *(AP/Wide World Photos)*

High School Athlete of the Year following his senior season.

Many colleges pursued him. Allen picked the University of Southern California because his football idol, O. J. Simpson, had gone there. During his senior year at USC, Allen had a record eight games in which he rushed for 200 yards or more. He finished the season with 2,342 rushing yards. Never before in NCAA (National Collegiate Athletic Association) history had a runner surpassed the 2,000-yard barrier. Allen was an easy winner in the Heisman Trophy voting.

When he became a pro player, the awards kept coming. Allen was the NFL's Rookie of the Year in 1982 and the league's Most Valuable Player in 1985. He holds the record for consecutive games rushing for 100 yards or more, with eleven. During his sixteen-year career Allen rushed for 12,243 yards, which is seventh on the all-time list.

Allen was a long-striding, graceful runner with great power and balance. This was due in part to the rigorous physical fitness program that he followed. Three times a week he did sit-ups, jumping jacks, squat thrusts, and fingertip push-ups. He also worked out on a four-inch balance beam, practicing kicking and walking. He did kicks at a ballet barre, too.

Allen wasn't merely a breakaway runner. He was well known for his ability to get the nasty yards. When the Raiders and, later, the Chiefs needed a yard or so for a first down or a touchdown, it would be Allen who would be sent hurtling into the line.

What was Allen's greatest day in football came in Super Bowl XVIII in 1984, the Raiders versus the Washington Redskins. Allen showed the way in the Raiders' 38–9

A graceful runner with exceptional cutback ability, Allen churns out yardage against the Cleveland Browns. *(AP/Wide World Photos)*

The Raiders defeated the Washington Redskins, 38–9, in Super Bowl XVIII. The game's MVP award went to Allen. *(AP/Wide World Photos)*

After eleven seasons with the Raiders, Allen finished his career with the Kansas City Chiefs.
(AP/Wide World Photos)

win, carrying the ball twenty times for 191 yards, the Super Bowl record. That total included a sensational 74-yard touchdown run. He walked away with MVP honors.

In a press conference after the game Allen was asked about his touchdown run. "Before the game, I actually pictured myself breaking free for a long run," he said. "But I didn't picture myself going in for a touchdown. The reality was better than the dream."

Besides his extraordinary achievements as a runner during his years as a professional, Allen also excelled as a pass receiver. In each of three consecutive seasons early in his career he caught at least sixty passes. And in each of those seasons he also rushed for one thousand yards or more.

When asked the reason for his success, Allen never cited his physical attributes. "My whole game is attitude," he said. "You've got to think positively to achieve the impossible, to be what you expect to be. If you seek mediocrity, that's what you get. I have a burning desire to be the best."

Earl Campbell

Born: March 29, 1955; Tyler, Texas
Height: 5' 11"   Weight: 230 lbs.
High School: John Tyler (Tyler)
College: University of Texas
Pro Teams: Houston Oilers, 1978–1984;
New Orleans Saints, 1984–1985
Entered Hall of Fame in 1991

"Bad Earl" he was called as a young teenager. The sixth of eleven children, Earl Campbell had a troubled childhood that was marked by long stretches of delinquency. Influenced by his deeply religious mother, Earl turned his life around during his high school years. He lifted himself up.

Later, as a pure power runner, he was Bad Earl to any opposing player that tried to bring him down. His massive forearms and thighs enabled him to overpower the biggest defenders. Gang tackling was the only way to stop him. In fourth-down and short-yardage situations, there was no one better.

Campbell's powerful running style produced some splendid results. At the University of Texas he led the Longhorns to an undefeated season in 1977 and won the Heisman Trophy as the nation's best college player.

Earl and his mother flew to New York for the presentation ceremony. Two former winners, Jay Berwanger and O. J. Simpson, handed the trophy

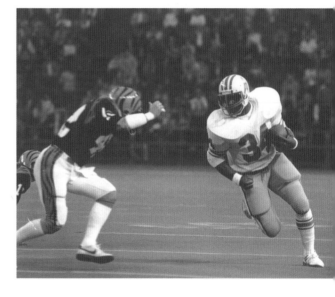

In 1978, his rookie year, Campbell ran for 1,450 yards, more than half of Houston's rushing yardage that season. *(AP/Wide World Photos)*

to Earl. His mother stood to one side, smiling. Earl had lifted himself up higher than she had ever hoped.

After college Earl signed a five-year, $1.4 million contract with the Houston Oilers. The Houston

(Left) Campbell was one of the most powerful and punishing runners in NFL history. Mel Blount of the Pittsburgh Steelers uses Campbell's jersey to try to bring him down. *(AP/Wide World Photos)*

(Below) The Oilers traded Campbell to the New Orleans Saints in 1984. After being cast in a backup role there, Campbell retired. *(AP/Wide World Photos)*

coach, O. A. "Bum" Phillips, revamped the Houston offense, installing formations designed to make the most of Earl's speed and punishing power.

The strategy worked. In 1978, his first season with the Oilers, Earl rushed for a league-leading 1,405 yards. The first rookie since Jim Brown to lead the NFL in rushing, he was the league's Rookie of the Year.

In 1980, his finest season, Earl rushed for 1,934 yards. At the time, that ranked as the third-best rushing performance in history. Earl was named Player of the Year in the NFL. Football people were saying that Earl might become the NFL's greatest running back of all time.

Despite such appraisals, Earl was not entirely comfortable in his career. The coaches wanted him to block more, and Earl was not especially skilled in blocking for other ballcarriers. They wanted him to circle out of the backfield and catch passes. Earl knew that he wasn't very good at that, either.

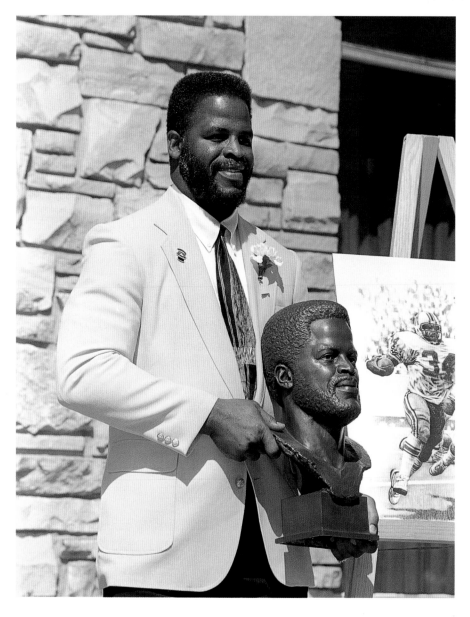

Campbell poses happily following his induction into the Pro Football Hall of Fame in 1991. *(AP/Wide World Photos)*

There was another problem. Because of his wondrous achievements as a runner, some people thought that Earl should be more of a leader. Quiet and soft-spoken, even shy, Earl did not feel that he wanted to play more of a leadership role.

"I don't talk enough to be a team leader," he told the *New York Times*. "I'm just not the guy. I'm not one to shuck and jive a lot. Oh, if this guy or that guy has problems, I'll listen. But I've got enough problems of my own."

His teammates understood Earl. They liked and respected him.

But Earl had disagreements with coaches. And the media sometimes questioned whether he always gave his best. Earl asked to be traded. The lack of team success—two wins, fourteen losses in 1983—contributed to Earl's frustrations.

In October 1984, Earl was dealt to the New Orleans Saints. He played two seasons for the Saints, then retired. He was only 593 yards short of 10,000 yards rushing for his career.

Earl Campbell made a substantial mark in pro football. He did in the world outside the sport too. He regularly set aside some of his salary for the Earl Campbell Crusade for Kids. The organization sought to help poor kids in Houston keep out of trouble—that is, to prevent the making of any more Bad Earls.

Tony Dorsett

Born: April 7, 1954; Rochester, Pennsylvania
Height: 5' 11"   Weight: 190 lbs.
High School: Hopewell (Aliquippa, Pennsylvania)
College: University of Pittsburgh
Pro Teams: Dallas Cowboys, 1977–1987; Denver Broncos, 1988
Entered Hall of Fame in 1994

When Tony Dorsett was growing up around Aliquippa, Pennsylvania, in the 1960s, his nickname was "Hawk." That was because of his big eyes.

Later, when he started playing football at the University of Pittsburgh, he was called "T. D." —short for Tony Dorsett and *touchdown*.

"T. D." really fit. Tony astounded people with his shifty moves and sprinter's speed. It was almost impossible to keep him out of the end zone. "Tony is quicker than a hiccup and tougher than week-old bread," said a Pittsburgh coach.

In 1976 Tony led Pittsburgh to an undefeated season and a victory over the University of Georgia in the Cotton Bowl. Sportswriters acclaimed the Panthers as college football's number one team. Tony, who set a helmetful of rushing records that season, won the Heisman Trophy as college football's outstanding player.

Whether getting a handoff from the quarterback or catching a pass, Dorsett ran with stunning speed.
(AP/Wide World Photos)

25

(Left) Dorsett limbers up before a game against the New York Giants at Giants Stadium. *(George Sullivan)*

(Below) Dorsett gets loose for a 99-yard touchdown run against the Minnesota Vikings on January 3, 1983. It was the longest run from scrimmage in NFL history. (AP/Wide World Photos)

Tony felt that the honor was deserved. "I think my statistics prove it," he said. He started wearing a gold medal engraved with No. 1 around his neck.

When he joined the Dallas Cowboys in 1977, it was more of the same. No one could run like Tony Dorsett. Although he didn't get into the starting line-up until the tenth game of the season, he still managed to rush for 1,007 yards and win Rookie of the Year honors.

Tony got even hotter in postseason play. By scoring four touchdowns in three play-off games, he helped boost the Cowboys into Super Bowl XII.

Some big players flop in big games. But not Tony Dorsett. He scored the game's first touch-down, and the Cowboys trimmed the Denver Broncos, 27–10.

"Tony is our catalyst," said Dallas coach Tom Landry. "He's the one that makes us go on offense."

In his first nine years with the Cowboys, Dorsett rushed for a thousand yards or more eight times. The only time he failed to reach that level was in 1982, when the football season was shortened to nine games by a players' strike. He also sparkled as a pass receiver, averaging thirty-seven catches a season.

Tony made football history on January 3, 1983, the last day of the regular NFL season. The Cowboys were playing the Minnesota Vikings in Minneapolis. After the Vikings scored a touchdown, the Cowboys fumbled the kickoff out of bounds on the one-yard line. On the next play the handoff went to Dorsett. He angled toward the sideline, then broke loose. Racing at top speed, he outran one tackler after another. He crossed into Viking territory and kept on speeding. One last Viking defender tried to shove him out of bounds, but Dorsett eluded him and crossed into the end zone. Tony's ninety-nine-yard gallop stands as the longest run from scrimmage in league history. Tony left the Cowboys for the Denver Broncos in 1988. He played one season for the Denver team. A knee injury forced him to retire in 1989.

But Tony could look back on a truly brilliant career. He played in two Super Bowls and five National Football Conference championship games. He's got a Super Bowl ring and a Heisman Trophy. He's got that line in the NFL record book that salutes his ninety-nine-yard touchdown run.

Dorsett's legacy also includes his son, Anthony, who joined the Houston Oilers in 1996 as a defensive back. The Dorsetts, Tony and Anthony, form one of a small handful of father-son combinations in the National Football League.

At five feet eleven inches, two hundred pounds, Anthony was about the same size as his dad. He went to the University of Pittsburgh, his dad's alma mater, and he wore the same uniform number, 33.

In 2000, after the Oilers had jumped to Nashville and become the Tennessee Titans, the team faced the St. Louis Rams in Super Bowl XXXIV. Anthony Dorsett started at safety for the team. He thus joined his dad in making NFL history as they became the first father and son each to play in the Super Bowl.

Dorsett played in two Super Bowls for the Cowboys, plus five conference championships and four Pro Bowls.
(George Sullivan)

Walter Payton

Born: July 25, 1954; Columbia, Mississippi
Height: 5' 10"   Weight: 200 lbs.
High School: Columbia
College: Jackson State University
Pro Team: Chicago Bears, 1975–1987
Entered Hall of Fame in 1993
Died: November 1, 1999

During his long and glittering career with the Chicago Bears, Walter Payton, known for his great power and unusual stiff-legged, high-stepping running style, was often hailed as the greatest runner of all time. There is plenty of evidence to support that opinion.

When "Sweetness," as he was nicknamed for his style both on and off the field, retired in 1987, he had accumulated 16,726 yards, which made him the greatest ground gainer in NFL history. The legendary Jim Brown was then second on the all-time list, and he was more than half a mile behind. In the late 1990s, Barry Sanders challenged the record. But the threat ended with Sanders's retirement in 1999.

Payton also held the record for one-hundred-yard rushing games, with seventy-seven, and thousand-rushing seasons, with ten. He was voted the league's Most Valuable Player in 1977 and 1985 and was named nine times to the Pro Bowl.

Payton was the kind of runner who punished

By the time his 13-year career had ended, Walter Payton's name dominated the NFL record book. (AP/Wide World Photos)

those who tried to tackle him. He would crash into defensive players with the force of an express bus or maul them with a powerful stiff-arm. He also excelled as a blocker. Running or blocking, Payton

left bruises on defensive players. Jack Young-blood, a onetime defensive end for the Rams, once recalled that Payton "rattled your teeth."

Payton's power was no accident. He spent count-less sweaty, painful hours developing his legs, hips, and upper body. He could bench-press 360 pounds and leg-press more than 600 pounds. Then there was the hill. In Arlington Heights, Illinois, not far from where Payton once lived, there was a black dirt hill, about 150 feet to the top and very steep. In preparing for a season he would run up and down the hill about twenty times a day. "I try to run on the hottest days at the hottest times," Payton said, "because that's more difficult."

Despite Payton's many contributions, the Bears were a mediocre team through most of his career. He often thought that he was never going to make it to the Super Bowl.

The Bears came close in 1984, Payton's tenth season with the club. Their quest was halted in

(Above)
When it came to physical fitness, Payton was always among the league leaders. *(AP/Wide World Photos)*

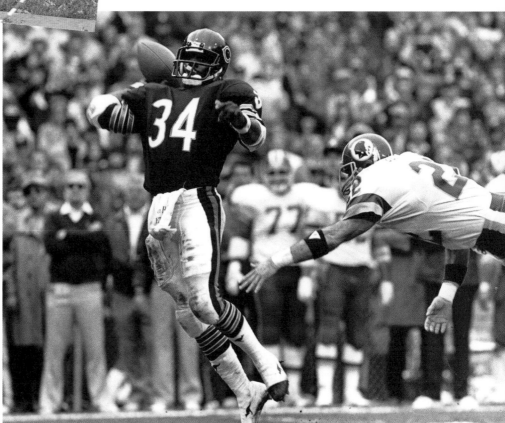

(Right) Payton not only carried the ball, occasionally he threw it. *(AP/Wide World Photos)*

Payton is congratulated by a teammate after setting the all-time game rushing record in November 1977. *(AP/Wide World Photos)*

ton had hoped for, because he did not score a touchdown.

"Are you disappointed?" he was asked at the postgame press conference.

"Disappointed? Yes, I'm disappointed," he said. "I feel bad. But that's the way the game goes. There were other games I didn't get into the end zone. But if they're keying on me, and it opens up holes for other people, that's okay. I don't mind being the rabbit."

Payton retired after the 1987 season. Before long he owned Walter Payton Power Equipment, Inc., which marketed the sale of construction cranes and aerial lifts. He operated Walter Payton's Roundhouse Complex, a cluster of banquet halls not far from Chicago. He was co-owner of an Indy-car racing team. He also found time for civic and charitable causes. He was active with the March of Dimes, the Illinois Mental Health Association, the Boy Scouts, and the United Way. As a businessman he proved to be just as impressive as he had been as a running back.

the conference title game, when they lost to the 49ers.

But the very next season, with Payton becoming the first running back in history to surpass fifteen thousand yards rushing, the Bears won the conference championship and a chance to play in Super Bowl XX. The New England Patriots provided the opposition. It was a romp for the Bears. They won, 46–10.

The outcome, however, was not quite what Pay-

When Payton died of cancer and a rare liver disease in 1999, it sent shock waves through the world of professional football. Flags flew at half-staff at Soldier Field in Chicago, and NFL Commissioner Paul Tagliabue hailed Payton not only as "a warrior on the field," but also as "an inspiration in everything he did."

Franco Harris

Born: March 7, 1950; Mount Holly, New Jersey
Height: 6' 2"   Weight: 230 lbs.
High School: Rancocas Valley Regional (Mount Holly)
College: Pennsylvania State University
Pro Teams: Pittsburgh Steelers, 1972–1983; Seattle Seahawks, 1984
Entered Hall of Fame in 1990

Franco Harris's most famous play was not a run, but a catch. It came in a play-off game between the Pittsburgh Steelers and the Oakland Raiders two days before Christmas in 1972, Franco's rookie year with the club. The Steelers trailed, 7–6, with only twenty-two seconds remaining in the game.

Pittsburgh had the ball on their forty-yard line. It was fourth down and ten yards to go. If the Steelers did not get at least a first down, their dreams of a conference championship would be shattered.

Quarterback Terry Bradshaw had no choice but to put the ball in the air. As he dropped back, Oakland linemen stormed in. Squirming away from a Raider tackler, Bradshaw darted to his left, then back to his right. Finally

Harris goes outside for a 6-yard gain against the Browns. Clarence Scott is the Cleveland defender. *(AP/Wide World Photos)*

31

Bradshaw stopped running, cocked his arm, and fired the ball to running back Jack Fuqua. But Oakland safety Jack Tatum raced toward Fuqua and got a hand on the ball, which struck someone's shoulder and caromed into the air.

Franco Harris saw it all. He saw the ball pop into the air and then start falling toward the ground. But it never hit the ground. Exploding toward the ball, bending as he ran, Franco scooped it up at just below knee level. Then, without breaking stride, he sprinted into the end zone.

The Steelers had always been a lowly team. They had never won a championship of any kind. With Franco's miraculous catch they had beaten the Raiders, 13–7, and had finally captured a division title.

The Steelers didn't get to the Super Bowl that year, but they went on to become pro football's most formidable team of the 1970s, winning four Super Bowls. Franco Harris contributed with his shifty, breakaway gallops. In eight of his twelve seasons with the Steelers he ran for at least a thousand yards.

Franco always seemed to raise the level of his game for the play-offs. In thirteen of the nineteen postseason games in which he took part, Franco was the leading rusher. In 1975, against the Vikings in Super Bowl IX, Franco was never better, gaining a record 158 yards on thirty-four carries. He was named the game's Most Valuable Player.

"We had a lot of stars, but none dwarfed Franco," Dwight White, a defensive lineman for the

Taking Terry Bradshaw's handoff, Harris darts for a hole in the New York Giants's line. *(George Sullivan)*

(Left) Harris gets wrapped up after a short gain against the Houston Oilers. (AP/Wide World Photos)

(Below) Harris not only had breakaway speed, he had the power to get the tough yards between tackles. (AP/Wide World Photos)

Steelers and a teammate of Franco's for nine years, told the *New York Times*. "He was always *the* man."

At six feet two, 230 pounds, Harris had the size of a fullback. But he didn't barrel straight ahead like a standard fullback. With his remarkable quickness and balance, and his ability to cut "against the grain" to either the right or left, Franco was as elusive as a slimmer halfback.

After the 1983 season Franco needed only 363 yards to break pro football's career rushing record of 12,312 yards, then held by Jim Brown. But the Steelers and Franco were not able to come to terms. Franco spent his final season with the Seattle Seahawks, where he was seldom used. At the time he retired, Franco was within 192 yards of Brown's record.

Quiet and dignified, with a pleasing personality, Franco became a business success and noted civic figure in Pittsburgh. He worked diligently for Children's Hospital and other charities. He received the 1982 Byron "Whizzer" White Humanitarian Award and overall as many honors as he had ever won on the football field.

But it is not for what he accomplished as a businessman or as a running back that Franco Harris is remembered. It is for the Catch, the Immaculate Reception, as it came to be called. By 1997, the twenty-fifth anniversary of the feat, it had won recognition as the most publicized play in American sport.

John Riggins

Born: August 4, 1949; Seneca, Kansas
Height: 6' 2"   Weight: 230 lbs.
High School: Centralia (Kansas)
College: University of Kansas
Pro Teams: New York Jets, 1971–1975;
Washington Redskins, 1976–1979, 1981–1985
Entered Hall of Fame in 1992

John Riggins had two careers in pro football, not merely one. In career number one, Riggins was a 230-pound ballcarrier and pass receiver for the New York Jets, an impressive runner with surprising speed.

After five years with the New York team Riggins moved on to the Washington Redskins as a free agent. Career number two was very different. With the Redskins, Riggins was a 245-pound short-yardage runner, one of the most successful in pro football history. In third-and-one situations he was nearly impossible to stop.

Washington fans that watched Riggins plow into the middle of the line on play after play probably never realized that he had once been quite a speedster. At Centralia (Kansas) High School, Riggins was twice the state champion in the hundred-yard dash. And at the University of Kansas, Riggins broke season and career rushing records that had been held by fleet-footed Gale Sayers.

After being drafted by the Jets in 1971, Riggins became the team's star running back. With the Redskins he was both a star and a hero.

Riggins's most spectacular act of heroics came in 1983 in Super Bowl XVII against the Miami Dolphins. The Dolphins led, 17–13, in the fourth quarter. The Redskins had the ball on the Dolphins' forty-three-yard line. It was fourth down and one yard to go for a first down. Every person in the crowd of 103,667 knew that Riggins was going to get the ball.

And he did. He took a handoff from quarterback Joe Theismann, but instead of hurtling into the middle of the line for that needed yard as the defense surely expected him to do, Riggins veered to his left and hurried around the end. It was then clear sailing to the end zone, except for one player. Riggins shifted into high gear and outran him.

The Redskins scored another touchdown later in the quarter. That made the final score Redskins, 27; Dolphins, 17. It was Washington's first NFL title since 1942. In the team's only other Super

With the New York Jets, Riggins often displayed speed and agility. *(George Sullivan)*

Bowl appearance, ten years earlier, the Redskins had lost to the Dolphins.

It was agreed that Riggins's forty-three-yard rumble had settled the game. At the time, it was the longest touchdown run in Super Bowl history. Riggins finished the game with 166 yards rushing. He was named the game's Most Valuable Player.

President Ronald Reagan certainly agreed with the MVP balloting. When he called Washington coach Joe Gibbs to congratulate the team, the president joked that he was considering changing the spelling of his name to "Reaggins."

Riggins later said that the game changed his life in several different ways: "One of them was that it made Washington kind of a small town for me, like Centralia all over again. I'd walk down the street and people would be calling, 'Riggio.'

"You have to remember," Riggins added, "Washington had only two things that most of the people there care about. The government and the Redskins, and a lot of the time they don't care about the government."

Riggins played a couple of years more for the

Riggins watches from the sidelines as the Dolphins crush the Jets. *(George Sullivan)*

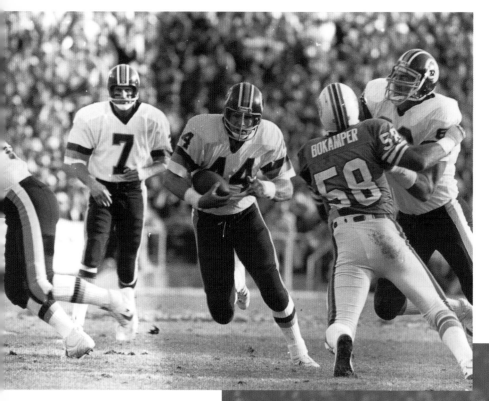

(Left) Riggins cruises for a long gain against the Miami Dolphins in Super Bowl XVII. With 166 yards rushing, Riggins earned MVP honors.
(AP/Wide World Photos)

(Below) Riggins goes over the top to score against the San Francisco 49ers.
(AP/Wide World Photos)

Redskins, then retired. His career had covered fourteen seasons, exceptionally long for a running back, given the beating they take. In total, he had five seasons in which he rushed for 1,000 yards or more. Riggins once noted that he was, at thirty-five, the oldest running back in history to gain 1,000 yards. (In 1984 he rushed for 1,289 yards.) At the time of his retirement, Riggins, with 104 touchdowns rushing, was third on the all-time list, behind Jim Brown and Walter Payton.

After retiring from football, Riggins had a radio talk show in Washington and worked as a sports broadcaster. "An entertainer" is what he called himself, and noted, "That's what a football player is, isn't it?"

O. J. Simpson

Born: July 9, 1947; San Francisco, California
Height: 6' 1"   Weight: 210 lbs.
High School: Galileo (San Francisco)
Colleges: City College of San Francisco,
University of Southern California
Pro Teams: Buffalo Bills, 1969–1977; San
Francisco 49ers, 1978–1979
Entered Hall of Fame in 1985

"The Year of the Running Back." That's what football people called 1972. Runners went wild that season.

Ten running backs gained one thousand yards or more in 1972, an extraordinary showing. In the five previous NFL seasons only fourteen runners had managed to exceed the thousand-yard mark.

A rule change was one reason for the remarkable running that season. The two sets of inbounds lines from which plays begin were moved closer to the center of the field. This caused defense to spread out and gave rushers more running room.

In the Year of the Runner, O. J. (for Orenthal James) Simpson was number one. With 1,231 yards rushing, "the Juice," as he was called, outgained every other runner on the planet.

The season of 1972 was O. J.'s fourth in professional football. The years preceding

During his career, O. J. was hailed by the *New York Times* as "the most talented running back the game has ever known." *(George Sullivan)*

had been mostly dismal for him. O. J. had signed with the Buffalo Bills after an exceptional college career at the University of Southern California. With his great speed and ability to cut, fake, and wriggle through the line, Simpson had won the Heisman Trophy during his senior year. He was also voted the College Player of the Decade, the decade being the 1960s.

All of these triumphs did not mean much to John Rauch, coach of the Bills. "I'm not going to build my offense around one back no matter how good he is," said Rauch.

Change came in 1972, when Lou Saban took over as coach. Saban acquired some big, agile linemen to block for O. J. And he installed running plays that got O. J. to the outside, where he could turn on his speed, toss in a stutter step or two, and be off for a big gain. O. J. liked to be able to go one-on-one with a safety. He liked to be able to "put a wiggle on him" or give the man a stiff-arm. "Once I get there," O. J. said, "it's my game."

O. J. had a good season in 1972 under Saban, but 1973 was even better. With one game remaining on the Buffalo schedule, O. J. needed only 61 yards to surpass Jim Brown's season record of 1,863 yards rushing.

The Bills traveled to New York City to play the Jets. The day was cold and dreary. Not long before the kickoff it started snowing. The conditions didn't bother O. J. Late in the first period, on his eighth carry, he followed a blocker through the left side of the line for a gain of six yards, which put him over the top. He had broken Brown's record.

O. J. wasn't through, however. When the second half began, his teammates in the offensive line began thinking that with their help O.J. might be able to hike his total to 2,000 yards and beyond for the season. At the time, no runner had ever surpassed 2,000 yards.

The historic moment arrived with six minutes, twenty-eight seconds remaining. O. J. drove into the

O. J. takes an outside route against the New York Jets. *(George Sullivan)*

When Simpson was a sprinter at the University of Southern California, his hard-muscled legs carried him through the 100-yard dash in 9.4 seconds. *(George Sullivan)*

After football, O. J. enjoyed a highly successful career in films and television. In the movie Capricorn One, he played an astronaut. *(AP/Wide World Photos)*

left side of the line for 7 yards. That boosted his total to 2,003 yards. O. J.'s teammates hoisted him to their shoulders and paraded him around the field. O. J. raised a fist in triumph.

Although he played in Buffalo for another four seasons, that was O. J.'s golden moment in pro football. After the Bills, O. J. spent two seasons with the 49ers. Bad knees hobbled him there. He retired after the 1979 season. Once he left football, O. J. had a high-profile career in the movies and as a TV broadcaster.

Mention O. J. Simpson today and hardly anyone thinks of the Heisman Trophy that he won, his four NFL rushing titles, or his super season of 1973, when he became the first runner in history to break the two-thousand-yard barrier.

Talk about O. J. today and people think of the June 1994 murders of his wife and her friend. O. J. was accused of the killings. A sensational murder trial followed. O. J. was acquitted of criminal charges, but a civil jury later found him liable for the crimes.

Millions remember "the Trial of the Century," as the criminal trial was called. Only a handful can or want to recall the Year of the Runner and O. J.'s exploits that year. All those football achievements don't seem very important anymore.

Gale Sayers

Born: May 30, 1943; Wichita, Kansas
Height: 6'   Weight: 195 lbs.
High School: Central (Omaha, Nebraska)
College: University of Kansas
Pro Team: Chicago Bears, 1965–1971
Entered Hall of Fame in 1977

During the 1950s a new system of blocking was introduced. Called option blocking, it was meant to put more zip into the running game.

Option blocking gave an offensive lineman the option—or choice—of blocking the defensive player across the line to either the right or left, whichever seemed best. If the defensive man wanted to go to the left, the offensive man would drive the man in that direction.

It was then up to the ballcarrier to "read" what was taking place and react accordingly. When the offensive lineman moved the defensive player he was blocking to the left, the runner would dart to the right, where an opening had been created. This was called "running to daylight."

Gale Sayers, a rookie with the Chicago Bears in 1965, ran to daylight, and he did it better than anyone else. He had dazzling

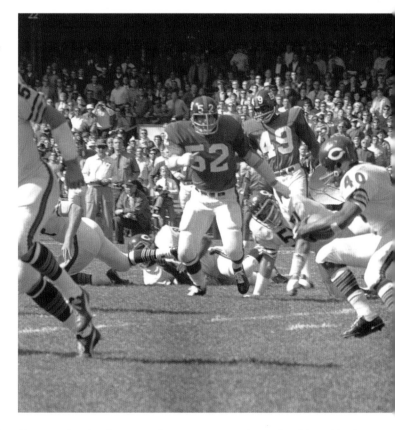

Sayers looks for running room against the New York Giants. *(George Sullivan)*

*(Left)*Sayers explores the end zone before a game against the New York Giants at Yankee Stadium. *(George Sullivan)*

(Below) Sayers is carried from the field after suffering torn ligaments in his right knee in a game against the San Francisco 49ers in 1968. *(AP/Wide World Photos)*

speed. He had incredible moves. He was, without any doubt, the greatest breakaway runner of his time—maybe of all time.

Sayers had a run-to-daylight philosophy. "In my book, the first objective is always getting the TD," he said. "It's nice to get the first and ten, but I'm looking for the TDs, and the first downs come second."

With that point of view and his exceptional talents, the six-foot, 195-pound Sayers had one spectacular game after another during his rookie year. By the season's end he was a superstar.

Sayers's greatest day as a rookie came in a game against the 49ers. Following his TD philosophy, he broke loose for runs of fifty, eighty, and eighty-five yards. Each resulted in a touchdown. In all, he scored six touchdowns that afternoon. Only twice before in NFL history had a player scored six touchdowns in a game. Never before had a rookie done it.

Coaches around the league sought to adjust their defense to put the brakes on Sayers. They weren't very successful. In his sophomore season Sayers led the league in rushing with 1,231 yards.

Sayers's ability to detect daylight was apparent in a simple off-tackle power play that the Bears liked to run. "I have the option of cutting in one of three directions," Sayers said. "If the guard knocks his man inside, I can go outside. If he knocks him outside, I can go inside. And if we're going for a first down, I can always blast straight ahead."

Injuries were what finally slowed down Gale Sayers. In a game against the 49ers at Wrigley Field in Chicago in November 1968, Sayers gathered in a pitchout and headed to his left. Just as he planted his right foot, a tackler chopped him down. The impact tore ligaments in Sayers's right knee, ending his season. Surgery followed and then a long and painful period of rehabilitation.

Sayers's attempt at a comeback was successful—by most standards. In 1969, the season after his injury, Sayers led the league in rushing again, with 1,032 yards. But the season was a disappointment to him because he realized he lacked the great speed he once had.

Then Sayers was cut down a second time in 1970. This time his other knee, the left knee, was the one that was injured. There was more surgery, more agonizing rehabilitation.

Sayers made a second comeback attempt in 1971, but it was less successful than the first. It was obvious that his ability to cut and fake, to blaze away from a tackler, had been diminished. His friends told him that he should think about leaving the game.

Sayers's final appearance on the football field came in a preseason game in 1972. He made three attempts at carrying the ball. He fumbled twice.

After the game Sayers was downcast. "I knew what I wanted to do," he said. "But I couldn't do it. I'd better give it up." Shortly after, Sayers retired.

Gale Sayers's career lasted seven seasons, a total of sixty-eight games. "He is the greatest football player I have ever seen," a teammate, tight end Mike Ditka, said of him. Had Gale Sayers not been injured, there's no telling what he might have been able to achieve.

The Bears retired Sayers's uniform number in ceremonies at Soldier Field in Chicago in 1994. *(AP/Wide World Photos)*

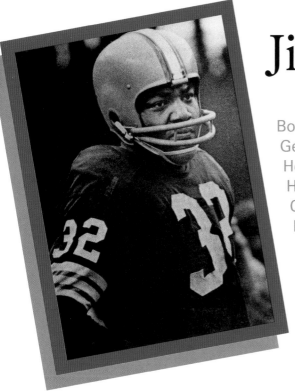

Jim Brown

Born: February 17, 1936; St. Simons Island, Georgia
Height: 6' 2"   Weight: 230 lbs.
High School: Manhasset (New York)
College: Syracuse University
Pro Team: Cleveland Browns, 1957–1965
Entered Hall of Fame in 1971

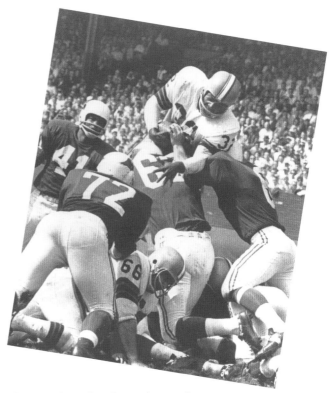

Brown hurdles into the end zone for a touchdown against the St. Louis Cardinals. *(AP/Wide World Photos)*

In 1965, as he entered his ninth and what would be his final season in professional football, Jim Brown, the most awesome runner the game had known, kept rewriting the record book. Every time he gained a yard, he broke his own all-time rushing record. If he caught a pass or returned a punt or kickoff, he set a new mark for total yardage. Every touchdown was a new high.

"Jimmy Brown is the best runner ever," said Ray Nitschke, a linebacker for the Green Bay Packers and often a rival of Brown's. "He not only had speed, power, and stamina. He had great intelligence. He always knew where he was going and how he was going to get there."

Brown was exceptionally powerful, a punishing runner, the ideal fullback. It almost always took two men to bring him down. But, like a halfback, he also had breakaway speed.

When he carried the ball, Brown was always sliding, adjusting, positioning himself for the blow that was to come. "The things you must avoid," he said, "are those shoulders in the midsection and collisions head-on. You have to sense what's dangerous."

Whenever Brown was tackled, he got up slowly and took his time going back to the huddle. He was once asked why he did this. "I like to have a

43

Brown rambles for 65 yards and a touchdown with the New York Giants tacklers in pursuit. *(AP/Wide World Photos)*

Through the years, a good number of running backs—including O. J. Simpson, Franco Harris, and Marcus Allen—have worn number thirty-two in Brown's honor. *(CBS-TV)*

man think that he might have hurt me," he said. "That makes it hard for the other fellow to know when I'm really hurt. It keeps them guessing."

Jim Brown was talented in many different sports. Football happened to be his career choice. At Manhasset High School he excelled in track and field. He pitched and played first base for the baseball team. He starred in lacrosse. He set rushing records in football. Forty-five colleges offered him scholarships. At Syracuse he continued his excellence in a variety of sports. In football he won all-American honors.

In 1957, his first season with the Browns, Brown led the NFL in rushing and was voted Rookie of the Year. He went on to lead the league's rushers in eight of his nine seasons. His average per carry of 5.2 yards and his five seasons as league leader in touchdowns are still records. He played in the Pro Bowl nine times, and he was the NFL's Most Valuable Player in 1958 and 1965. He never missed a game because of injury.

Despite Brown's efforts, the NFL championship kept eluding the Browns. His critics said that Brown himself was the reason. The Browns would never win a title with Brown, they claimed, because he wasn't a team player.

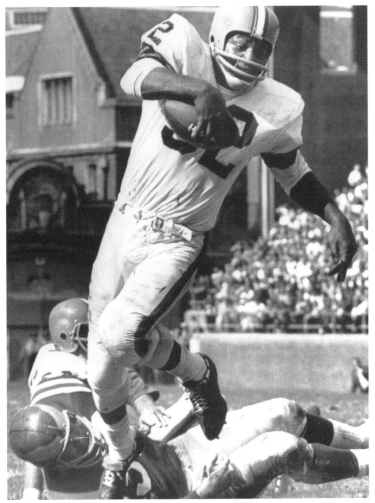

Brown surges into the end zone for 4 yards and a touchdown against the Philadelphia Eagles in 1965. It was his 106th touchdown, breaking the NFL record for career touchdowns. *(AP/Wide World Photos)*

Brown has a word for the audience following induction ceremonies at the Pro Football Hall of Fame in 1971. *(George Sullivan)*

In 1964 Brown stilled the critics. Cleveland faced the Baltimore Colts in the championship game that year. (There was as yet no Super Bowl.) The Colts were heavily favored. But the Cleveland defense kept the pressure on Baltimore quarterback Johnny Unitas, cutting his effectiveness. At halftime the game was scoreless.

In the third quarter Brown circled left end and got loose on a long run that set up a Cleveland field goal, the game's first score. When Cleveland got the ball back, Brown, taking a pitchout, broke into the open again for a forty-six-yard gain. Quarterback Frank Ryan then hit receiver Gary Collins with a scoring pass. The game ended with the Browns on top, 27–0. Brown played a vital role in the win, gaining 114 yards on twenty-seven carries.

Brown decided the 1965 season would be his last. He was twenty-nine. He obviously still had several good years ahead of him.

Why did he retire? "I saw athletes who stayed too long," he said. "I didn't want to become a second-stringer, a role player. I wanted to do something high profile."

Brown accomplished that. After he stepped down as an athlete, Brown made a number of action movies. He often spoke out on African-American issues. He raised questions about more coaching and executive jobs for minorities in the NFL. He was sometimes critical of other African-American superstars, such as Michael Jordan and Tiger Woods, for not buying businesses that could serve to expand black leadership. Jim Brown was still a presence.

Marion Motley

Born: June 5, 1920; Leesburg, Georgia
Height: 6' 1"   Weight: 230 lbs.
High School: McKinley (Canton, Ohio)
Colleges: South Carolina State University;
University of Nevada, Reno
Pro Teams: Cleveland Browns (AAFC),
1946–1949; Cleveland Browns (NFL),
1950–1953; Pittsburgh Steelers, 1955
Entered Hall of Fame in 1968
Died: June 27, 1999

Big, fast, and very powerful, Marion Motley was one of pro football's best fullbacks ever. He was also considered by many to be one of the greatest all-around players the game has known.

Motley's first four seasons with the Cleveland Browns were during the years that the team belonged to the All-America Football Conference, which operated from 1946–1949. In those four years the Browns were one of the winningest teams of all time. Of the fifty-four games that they played, they won forty-seven, lost four, and tied three. Never once did they fail to win the league championship.

When the AAFC folded in 1950, Motley was the league's career rushing leader, with 3,024 yards. The Browns (along with the Baltimore Colts and San Francisco 49ers) were then taken into the National Football League.

Many people believed that the Browns would be outclassed in the NFL. It never happened. The

His size and strength enabled Motley to achieve a remarkable 5.7 yards-per-carry average during his career. *(AP/Wide World Photos)*

Browns kept right on winning. Year in, year out, the Browns captured their conference title. They won the NFL championship in 1950. Motley led

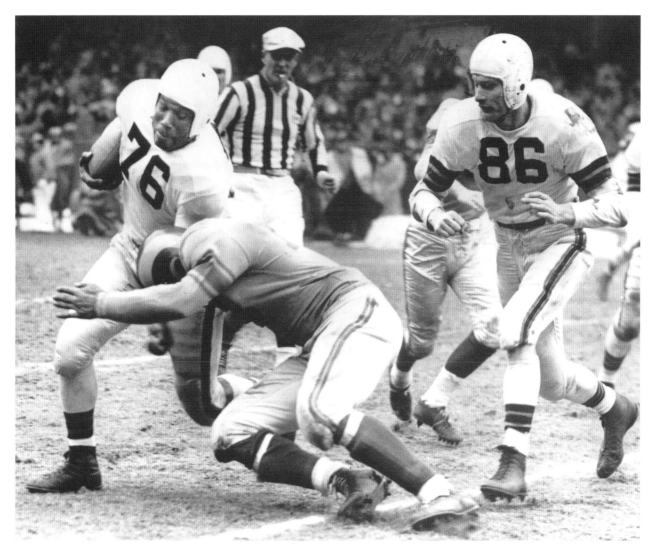

Motley picks up 12 yards and a first down against the Los Angeles Rams in the NFL title game in 1950. *(AP/Wide World Photos)*

the league in rushing that season, gaining 810 yards on 140 carries.

These numbers may seem low when compared to those of players who came later, but Motley's yards were tough yards. Although he had the speed to go outside, he wasn't sent wide very often. And by today's standards Motley was used sparingly as a runner. Terrell Davis or Barry Sanders carries the ball thirty times or so in a game. Motley averaged about nine or ten carries. The Browns, with Hall of Famer Otto Graham passing to a corps of standout receivers, preferred the pass to the run.

"There's no telling how much yardage I might have made if I ran as much as some backs do now," Motley once said.

This shouldn't imply that Motley was not busy. He was an exceptional pass blocker for Graham. And when the opposition had the ball, Motley played linebacker. He was a two-way player at a time when the rest of professional football was switching to separate offensive and defensive platoons.

"He was the greatest all-around player I ever saw," Blanton Collier, a coach of the Cleveland Browns, once told Paul Zimmerman of *Sports Illustrated*.

Coach Paul Brown once said of Motley, "Not only was he a great runner, but also no one blocked better—and no one cared more about the team." *(AP/Wide World Photos)*

Motley later found out that the Browns weren't particularly interested in his talents as a fullback, but his status quickly changed. In the opening game of Motley's rookie season in 1946, the team's starting fullback hurt his knee. Motley took over and soon became a fixture.

In a game for the AAFC title in 1947 Motley had a typical day. The Browns faced the New York Yankees (yes, the football Yankees) at Yankee Stadium. Motley gained 109 yards on thirteen carries. His longest run, fifty-one yards, came on a play that started up the middle. He struggled for the last ten yards or so because he had New York's Harmon Rowe clinging to his back and smacking him in the face.

After the game a photographer asked him to smile.

"I can't," Motley said. "They knocked out my front teeth."

That was only one of his problems. Motley had knee trouble in the last four seasons of his career and quit just before the 1954 season. He sought to restart his career with the Steelers in 1955. He played in a few games, but his bad knees prevented him from performing as he once had.

"The man was a great, great linebacker. Believe me, he could do everything. He had no equal as a blocker. Yes, he could do it all."

Motley's career as a college player gave little hint of the greatness he was to achieve as a professional. He was not even drafted by a pro team. After college he joined the navy.

After the navy, Motley planned to go back to college and get his degree. But the Browns offered him a job.

After his playing days Motley did some scouting for the Browns. He wanted to coach in the NFL, but in the 1950s and 1960s there were, unfortunately, very few coaching opportunities for former players who happened to be black.

In 1968 Motley was voted into the Pro Football Hall of Fame. Emlen Tunnell of the Giants was the first black player to achieve that honor. Marion Motley was the second.

Bronko Nagurski

Born: November 3, 1908; Rainy River, Ontario (Canada)
Height: 6' 2"   Weight: 225 lbs.
High Schools: Bemidji (Minnesota),
International Falls (Minnesota)
College: University of Minnesota
Pro Team: Chicago Bears, 1930–1937, 1943
Entered Hall of Fame in 1963
Died: January 7, 1990

Big running backs have been a part of pro football from its earliest days. Jim Thorpe and Ernie Nevers were two of them. Then there was Bronko Nagurski. At six feet two and 225 pounds, Nagurski may not have been so big by today's standards, but he was *really* big, a monster, in his time. Had he had the benefit of modern players' diet and weight training, Nagurski probably would have played at 275 pounds.

Besides being unusually big, Nagurski was very powerful. He ran headfirst, his knees pounding high. It was said that Nagurski didn't need any players running interference for him; he created his own.

"If you went at him low, he would stomp you to death," Mel Hein, an all-pro center for the Giants, once said. "And if you went at him high, he just knocked you down and ran over you."

Johnny Dell Isola, who backed up the line for the New York Giants, once recalled what it was like to tackle Nagurski. The Bears had the ball. It was

Nagurski streaks for yardage against the Washington Redskins in the NFL championship game in 1937. Redskins won, 28–21. *(AP/Wide World Photos)*

Nagurski uses a shoulder toss to overturn a teammate during a team workout. *(AP/Wide World Photos)*

first and ten. Nagurski took a handoff and barreled toward a hole that had been opened for him in the center of the line. Isola charged forward to fill the gap. "It was the hardest tackle I ever made," Isola said. "I remember saying to myself, 'I guess that will show you, Nagurski.' But as the officials were unpiling us, I heard the referee turn to the Bears and say, 'Second down and two.'" Nagurski had picked up eight yards on the play!

Like most players of the time, Nagurski played sixty minutes of every game. On defense he was a linebacker and, later, a tackle. He used what he called a "flying block" to bring down a ballcarrier, flinging his body crosswise at the runner's legs. It was like being hit across the knees with a telephone pole.

With the powerful Nagurski throwing those blocks and punching holes in enemy lines, the Bears won Western Division titles in 1933, 1934,

and 1937. They captured the league title in 1933 by defeating the New York Giants.

During this time Nagurski often squabbled with George Halas, the owner of the Bears, over money. In 1937 Nagurski had to threaten to retire in order to get his salary raised to $5,000. In 1938 he asked for an additional $1,000. When Halas refused, Nagurski quit.

Nagurski didn't lack for income. At the same time he was playing professional football, he was also pursuing a career as a professional wrestler. He was famous for the fierce flying block that he would launch at ring opponents.

During World War II, when pro football suffered a manpower shortage, George Halas asked the thirty-four-year-old Nagurski to return to the Bears, and he did. When the Bears faced the Washington Redskins for the NFL championship in 1943, it was Nagurski's touchdown plunge from

(Left) A "straight downfield runner" is how Nagurski described himself. "I wouldn't, or rather, couldn't, dodge anybody," he said. (Pro Football Hall of Fame)

(Below) As a professional wrestler, Nagurski twice claimed the world championship. (AP/Wide World Photos)

the three-yard line that broke a 7–7 tie and gave the Bears the edge at halftime. Chicago dominated the second half to win, 41–21.

After that Nagurski quit football for good, but he continued wrestling until 1960. In retirement Nagurski lived in International Falls, Minnesota. A kind and gentle man, he liked to hunt and fish in his spare time.

Sometimes he reminisced upon his days in pro football. He liked to remind listeners that he arrived upon the pro scene well before the modern era of the specialist on offense and defense.

"I could have played twenty more years if we'd had the platoon system in those days," he said. "But we had a lot more fun. The way it is now a fellow sits on the bench too much. I wouldn't have liked that."

Ernie Nevers

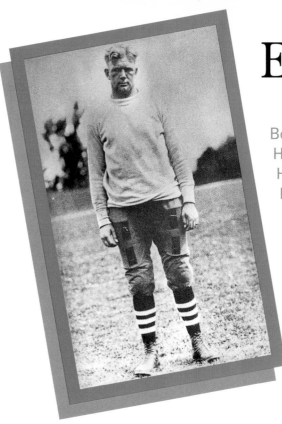

Born: June 11, 1903; Willow River, Minnesota
Height: 6' 4"   Weight: 205 lbs.
High Schools: Superior (Wisconsin) Central, Santa
Rosa (California)
College: Stanford University
Pro Teams: Duluth Eskimos, 1926–1927; Chicago
Cardinals, 1929–1931
Entered Hall of Fame in 1963
Died: May 3, 1976

In the official National Football League record book there's an entry that reads: "Most Points, Game—40, Ernie Nevers, Chicago Cardinals vs. Chicago Bears, November 28, 1929 (six touchdowns, four points-after touchdown)."

The player who was responsible for that remarkable point-scoring spree looked like a Hollywood version of a fullback. He was tall, strong, blond, and very modest. And with his power, agility, and speed, Ernie Nevers was also about as unstoppable as any fullback ever. He was called "the Blond Bull."

After starring in football and baseball at Stanford University, Ernie, a pitcher, played three seasons of Major League Baseball for the St. Louis Browns before a sore pitching arm put an end to his baseball career. He then turned to pro football, signing with the Duluth Eskimos.

In 1926, his rookie season with the team, the Eskimos played twenty-eight games—nineteen as

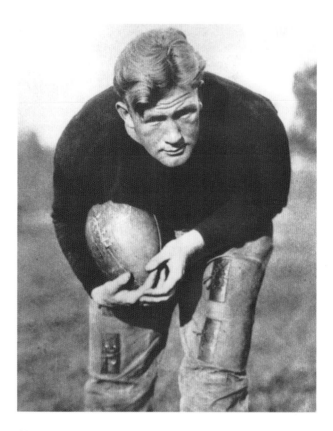

Nevers was called the "Iron Man." In 1926, during 28 games, he played all but 29 minutes. *(AP/Wide World Photos)*

part of the regular-season schedule and nine exhibition contests.

Because Ernie was one of the most celebrated college players of the time, the league made Ole Haugsrud, owner of the Eskimos, insert a clause in Nevers's contract saying that he would play a minimum of twenty-five minutes in each game. When Ernie heard about the clause, he was insulted. He felt it reflected on his integrity. Ernie intended to play both offense and defense, sixty minutes of every game, and he almost achieved that goal. In those twenty-eight games Ernie sat out a total of only twenty-nine minutes.

Money was scarce in pro football in those days. The budget for football talent was such that the Eskimos played their grueling schedule with a squad of only thirteen players. When the team went out onto the field before the game to warm up, the owner and the coach put on uniforms and ran around with the players. They wanted to prevent their opponents and the fans from realizing how pitifully undermanned they were.

Nevers rests his weary legs in 1929, the year he set his dazzling scoring record. *(Pro Football Hall of Fame)*

Nevers had many outstanding games with the Eskimos. One day, against Pottsville, Pennsylvania, he scored twenty-seven points. Another time, at Hartford, Connecticut, Nevers booted five field goals in a game.

Pro football franchises came and went with great frequency in the 1920s. The NFL had twenty-two teams in 1926. After that season ten clubs folded. The Duluth team lasted through 1927.

Ernie didn't play in 1928. Instead, he coached college football at Stanford. In 1929 Ernie signed with the Chicago Cardinals.

In the double-wing formation used by the Cardinals, Ernie, as the team's fullback, handled the ball on every play. He was not just the team's most dependable ballcarrier. He did the passing, punting, and placekicking. He also returned punts and kickoffs. He was the team's captain and eventually became its player-coach. Ernie did about everything except drive the team bus.

The game in which Ernie set the all-time scoring record was played against the Chicago Bears in Comiskey Park, where the city's American League baseball team, the White Sox, played their home games. It was also home grounds for the Cardinals.

It was freezing cold on the day of the game, and a fierce wind whipped the field. Although the city championship was at stake, only about eight thousand spectators turned out.

Because the field was frozen, the Cardinals weren't able to use their trick plays, which required quick shifts and elusive cuts. "All we could do," Nevers later recalled, "was shoot our power between tackles."

Ernie began the scoring in the first quarter with a twenty-yard touchdown gallop, his longest run of the day. His placekick attempt for the extra point went wide. Minutes later, Ernie scored a second touchdown on a five-yard plunge, then added the extra point. The Cards led, 13–0.

(Right) After he left professional football, Nevers (left) coached at Stanford University with the legendary Glenn (Pop) Warner. *(AP/Wide World Photos)*

(Below) Nevers did more than carry the ball; he also passed, placekicked, and punted. *(AP/Wide World Photos)*

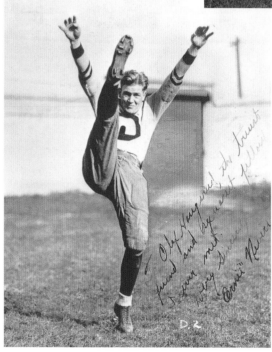

In the second quarter Ernie scored a third time by bulling into the end zone from the six-yard line. Again he added the extra point. That made the score 20–0, Cardinals.

In the third quarter Ernie rammed his way across the goal line from the one-yard line. His extra-point kick was good.

Ernie's fifth and sixth touchdowns came in the final period. One was the result of a one-yard plunge. The other came on a ten-yard run. A poor snap from center prevented an extra point after the fifth touchdown, but the other attempt was good.

Ernie's six touchdowns and four extra points added up to forty points. The final score: Cardinals, 40; Bears, 6.

Ernie's record has lasted for about three-quarters of a century. It was challenged by Chicago's Gale Sayers in a game against the 49ers in 1965, when Sayers scored six touchdowns—thirty-six points.

Nevers was watching on television that afternoon. With several minutes remaining Sayers was taken out of the game. Nevers was puzzled. "The Bears should have kept [Sayers] in," Nevers said after, "to let him try to break the forty-point record with another touchdown." In a similar situation you can be sure no one would have tried to take Ernie Nevers out.

Red Grange

Born: June 13, 1903; Forksville, Pennsylvania
Height: 6"   Weight: 180 lbs.
High School: Wheaton, Illinois
College: University of Illinois
Pro Teams: Chicago Bears, 1925, 1929–1934;
New York Yankees, 1926–1927
Entered Hall of Fame in 1963
Died: January 28, 1991

Harold "Red" Grange first earned headlines as a running back at the University of Illinois, where he astonished the world of sports in the 1920s with his explosive bursts of speed, fancy weaving, and long, electrifying runs. He moved, as sportswriter Grantland Rice once said, "as a shadow flits and drifts and darts." Rice nicknamed him "the Galloping Ghost."

One fall afternoon in 1924, in a game against the University of Michigan, he scored a touchdown each of the first four times he carried the ball. Later he scored a fifth touchdown and passed for a sixth. He was a three-time college all-American.

A few weeks after his final college game, Grange signed a contract with the Chicago Bears. People thought he was crazy. Major League Baseball and college football were the most popular sports of the time. Pro football was in a sorrowful state.

Colleges, especially, denounced the professionals. A college player who would take money for playing

Playing for the University of Illinois against the University of Michigan in 1924, Grange grabbed the game's opening kickoff and broke loose on a 95-yard touchdown run. *(AP/Wide World Photos)*

football was no longer pure, it was said. He had stained his character.

Grange shrugged off this criticism. "I see nothing wrong in playing pro football," he declared. "It's the same as playing professional baseball, it seems to me. I have to get the money now because people will forget about me in a few years."

Once George Halas, owner of the Bears, had Grange under contract, he wasted no time cashing in on his player's great popularity. He worked out an exhibition schedule that called for the team to play ten games in eighteen days. That was fine with Grange, who was to receive a percentage of the money taken in at the box office. He was also to receive a minimum of $3,000 a game, an extraordinary amount for the time. One newspaper kept a running account of the money that Grange earned.

The Bears and Grange played their first game against the Chicago Cardinals at Wrigley Field in Chicago on Thanksgiving Day in 1925. A sellout was the result. That had never happened before at a Bears-Cards game.

Within the next few days the Bears played in St. Louis and Philadelphia. The high point of the tour came when the Bears faced the New York Giants at the Polo Grounds in New York City. Grange's

Grange practices one of his fleet-footed moves during a Bears practice session. *(CBS-TV)*

Like other professionals of the time, Grange played on defense as well as offense. As a defensive back, he was acclaimed for his skill in intercepting passes. *(AP/Wide World Photos)*

popularity was such that by game time every seat had been sold and standing-room tickets were put on sale. An estimated seventy thousand fans watched Grange and the Bears that day, breaking all pro football attendance records.

The frantic tour continued. It was so successful that Halas booked another series of exhibition games for the Bears. This tour took the Bears into the major cites of Florida and the Pacific Coast.

For the pro season of 1926 Grange asked for a part interest in the Bears. Halas refused. That season Grange ended up playing for a New York team known as the Yankees.

In a game the following season Grange and the Yankees traveled to Chicago to play the Bears at Wrigley Field. Late in the game Grange collided with George Trafton, the Bears' huge center. When Grange went down, his cleats caught in the turf and he twisted his knee as he fell. Trafton landed on top of him.

Grange has some tips for youngsters attending a football instruction clinic in Chicago. *(AP/Wide World Photos)*

Grange was on crutches for four months as doctors sought to repair the damage to his knee. They were only partly successful. The injury robbed Grange of his great speed and elusiveness. "After it happened, I was just another halfback," Grange once said.

Grange continued to play, however. He returned to Halas and the Bears in 1929 and his career went on for another six seasons.

He was a member of the NFL's all-pro team as a halfback in 1931. In the league's championship game in 1932 he caught a pass from Bronko Nagurski and scored the winning touchdown. He retired after the season of 1934. During his retirement Grange was active in radio and TV, broadcasting Bears games. He lived in Florida.

Red Grange's name doesn't appear on the list of all-time leading rushers. It can't be found in the NFL record book, either. But as the first player whom great numbers of people were eager to pay to see, Red Grange had an important influence. People gained a greater appreciation for pro football because of Grange. He helped set the stage for the future growth of the game.

Jim Thorpe

Born: May 28, 1887; Prague, Oklahoma
Height: 6' 1"   Weight: 200 lbs.
High School: Haskell (Oklahoma) Indian Institute
College: Carlisle Indian School
Pro Teams: Canton Bulldogs, 1915–1920, 1926;
Cleveland Indians, 1921; Oorang Indians,
1922–1923; Rock Island Independents, 1924;
New York Giants, 1925; Chicago Cardinals, 1928
Entered Hall of Fame in 1963
Died: March 28, 1953

In the first years of its existence, the National Football League had a good number of heroes. The colleges, big and small, that specialized in football offered an endless supply of talent. Jim Thorpe, whose extraordinary feats in football, baseball, and track and field had earned him recognition as one of the best all-around athletes in history, was the biggest hero of them all.

Thorpe was twenty-seven years old when he signed his first pro football contract in 1915. He had won all-American honors at the Carlisle Indian School, where he led the football team to the national collegiate championship. He had captured gold medals in the five-event pentathlon and ten-event decathlon in the 1912 Olympic Games, setting records in both events. He had added to his fame by playing three years of Major League Baseball with the New York Giants.

In 1915, when Thorpe decided to give pro football a try, there was no National Football League,

Thorpe, it was said, could punt a football eighty yards and more. *(AP/Wide World Photos)*

Thorpe (lower right corner) poses with several members of the all-time, All America football team. Other players include Ernie Nevers (upper right corner). *(AP/Wide World Photos)*

no league of any kind. A handful of teams clustered in the small industrial towns of Ohio played the game for money. Thorpe's team was the Canton Bulldogs.

Thorpe was pro football's first "name" player. When his Canton team played their arch rivals, the Massillon Tigers, in 1916, some ten thousand fans turned out for the game, an enormous crowd for the time. The Bulldogs shut out the Tigers, 24–0. Afterward the team claimed to be champions of the pro football world, despite the lack of a structured league.

Thorpe, a halfback, was an awesome ballcarrier. "Jim had a way of running that I never saw before," said Pete Calac, a teammate of Thorpe's.

Not everyone wore helmets in those days, and Jim would shift his hip to-ward the guy about to tackle him, then swing it away. And then, when the player moved toward him, he'd swing the hip back, hard, against the tackler's head and leave him lying there.

He usually ran from the outside. That's what he liked—to get out there and use that shifty hip and wicked straight-arm.

Thorpe was a fierce defensive player, too. He wore special shoulder pads made of hard leather, and "they hit like iron," recalled George Halas, who played against him. "If he hit you from behind, he'd throw that big body across your back and about break you in two."

Thorpe was with Canton in 1920 when the owners of eight teams got together to form an organized league. They called it the American Professional Football Association. They elected Thorpe the league president. The next year Thorpe stepped down and a new president was chosen. In 1922 the league picked a new name: the National Football League (although it was hardly "national," since no teams were located west of the Mississippi River).

Thorpe's career in pro football continued for

most of the decade. He drifted from one team to another. In 1922 and 1923 he played for the Oorang Indians, a team that was organized to promote a La Rue, Ohio, dog kennel. The Indians won only three games in two years.

On November 29, 1929, Thanksgiving Day, the forty-two-year-old Thorpe made a brief appearance for the Chicago Cardinals in their traditional game against the Bears. According to the Associated Press, he was "muscle-bound" and "a mere

shadow of his former self." The next year Thorpe was out of pro football.

In 1950, when the Associated Press asked 393 sportswriters to name the outstanding athlete of the half century, Thorpe won with 252 first-place votes.

Upon Thorpe's death in 1953, the *New York Times* saluted him as "the greatest athlete of them all," and noted, "There seems to be general agreement that no one ever equaled him on the football gridiron."

Thorpe, at age sixty, jogs with youngsters in his role as a physical fitness instructor for the city of Chicago. *(AP/Wide World Photos)*